VOICES OF EXPERIENCE

A COMPILATION of
STORIES, ESSAYS AND POEMS
published by
THE SENIOR STUDIES INSTITUTE
to mark the bicentenary of
STRATHCLYDE UNIVERSITY

THE
UNIVERSITY OF
STRATHCLYDE
IN GLASGOW

Learning in
Later Life
Students' Association

SENIOR STUDIES
INSTITUTE

Photography; Val Bissland
Line Drawings; Laura Steele

ISBN 0 952 8158 0 X

The book is produced by:

gray's reproduction
production
graphics

41 Abercrombie Drive, North Baljaffray,
Bearsden, Glasgow G61 4RR
0141-942 5755

Preface

This is The Senior Studies Institute's first publication. The Institute invited writers from all over Scotland to contribute to this book, and received over two hundred entries. The standard was very high, making the choosing of the winner a daunting task, but the whole process has been extremely satisfying, largely because of the wealth of talent that has emerged.

To those who have worked so hard at turning an idea into something tangible and lasting, my appreciation and thanks are extended.

Lesley Hart (Head of the Senior Studies Institute), Ann Thomson (Chair of the Learning in Later Life Students' Association) and Archie Fleming (Director of the Continuing Education Centre) have given enormous support, and in so doing have upheld the spirit of innovation for which the S.S.I. has become internationally renowned.

The work of the Editorial Panel is also very much appreciated. Carl MacDougall, author, and Alan MacGillivray of the Department of English Studies willingly accepted the task of reading all the submissions and subsequently choosing the contents of the book.

Thanks are extended to Ian Gray, whose advice on the layout, printing and publishing has been generously given; to Val Bissland who put so much professional care and thought into the photography; and to art student Laura Steele, who created the illustrations.

Thanks also to Joy, Karen, and Sandra, of the S.S.I. office staff.

And finally to the writers, whose voices are being heard and whose experience has been skilfully woven into the stories, essays, and poems on these pages. Thank you for sending in your work. I hope that you enjoy seeing it in print, and may you, along with many others, find pleasure in reading Voices Of Experience.

Jenny Laurie
Managing Editor.

The Editorial Panel chose as the winning entry
Moyra McGavin's poem
The Glasgow Aunts
and as runner-up
Elisabeth Fry's short story
The Shopping Trip.

Foreword

by *Professor Sir Graham Hills,*
Principal of Strathclyde University, 1980 – 1991

I was pleased to be asked to write a foreword to this collection of essays, poems and short stories. I know them to be a testament to the creative thinking and open minds of a new generation of older students, and to a new sector of higher education no longer needing to apologise for its existence.

1996 is the European Year Of Lifelong Learning, and it coincides with the 200th anniversary of the death of John Anderson and the foundation of this, his university. He was seventy when he died — good going in those days — and active to the last. He was a radical, restless kind of person; and he was yet another gifted child of the Scottish Enlightenment, which was to change his world every bit as much as the IT revolution is changing ours.

It was one of those rare times which encouraged men and women to think the unthinkable. Scotsmen wrote and signed the Declaration of Independance. Cherished beliefs were abandoned. Orthodoxy might have been thought a sign of feebleness of spirit. Above all else, the closed privileged nature of education was challenged. John Anderson's challenge was to open up university education to all, to ordinary men and women regardless of their age and their circumstances. Education for the Third Age might be thought to have been born there and then, and also, therefore, to be celebrating its 200th anniversary now.

Of course the orthodox do not go quietly. Believers in old customs fight to the death to defend them. After all, it is their cosy world which is threatened. In time, therefore, the brave new world of John Anderson gave way to Victorian values of respectability and of back-to-basics, and to other ways of dividing and excluding various sections of society. It took two world wars to liberate women, and to widen access to higher education. Even now, two hundred years on, that battle is still not won.

For an example near to home we need only to look at the older universities and ancient colleges. Busily defending the status quo and their expensive ways, they brook no other form of education for the precocious young than the single subject honours degree, an English anachronism taught by scholars and scholarly researchers, and examined by the age-old method of written answers to written questions based solely on word-based knowledge.

And yet the world outside the cloisters, which all new graduates must sometime enter, has other goals and goes a different way. It is less concerned with the know-what than the know-how. Could it be that Britain's decline as an industrial nation is simply due to the know-what having been elevated too highly over the know-how? Why do we still resist the pocket calculator, or the friendly personal computer? Its memory is infinite compared to our own.

The **new** brave new world is full of competencies, a new description for the range of professional and intellectual skills of all kinds which deal with how to protect our environment, how to cure our diseases, how to feed the world, and how to develop ourselves. Real education is discovering what matters, what we can do, and how we can do it.

And is the educational establishment alive to this momentous paradigm shift? Is it welcoming it with open arms? Not a bit. Like all establishments, it stares fixedly at its glorious past, and fears its uncertain future.

I believe that one of the joys of the Third Age, and of Learning in Later Life, is that we begin the real education of ourselves, begin to live as human beings, begin to see that deeds indeed speak louder than words. This is why this deed of writing and compiling the essays, poems and stories, appeals to me. They owe their charm and their value to their immediacy, to their freshness and to their novelty. Their authors know how to write, how to command attention, how to amuse, and how to live. That iconoclast, John Anderson, would have approved. He was truly a person of his time, imbued with the belief that young or old, male or female, bigwig or small wig, we can all make the best of ourselves, now.

Professor Sir Graham Hills
Principal of Strathclyde University when The Senior Studies Institute was established in 1991

VOICES OF EXPERIENCE

CONTENTS

A
Bomber's Moon
1941

Our big chance of going to America was squashed. We were disconsolate, my friend Nessie and I. In one quick stroke of a pen our parents had demolished our castles in the air. Meeting Shirley Temple, Mickey Rooney, Spanky McFarlane and Alfalfa of "Our Gang" was never to be.

That morning, Mrs. McKenzie our teacher had explained that the American people, although they hoped that the Germans would not bomb women and children, wanted in their good hearts to gives homes to us for the duration of the war. We had to take forms to our mums and dads to be signed, scoring out a yes or no, giving the school permission to evacuate their little ones. In our innocence we thought that a big adventure was in front of us and that War was going to be fun.

"Ye've tae sign that, Mammy!"

"Sign whit?"

My mother was dishing out the mid-day meal for the six of us. The seventh, my brother, was already in the army.

"This form. Ah'm gaun tae America! For the duration of the war!"

I did not know the meaning of those words.

My father, sitting at the head of the table, took the paper and read it. When my mother sat down, he quietly handed it over to her.

"It's too faur, Dick," she said, "Ah couldnae bear it."

I bristled. She was going to boss him as she always did.

"Yer mammy's right, pet."

"That's it then?"

Turning to me, her hazel eyes darkened.

"Ye're gaun nae place — we're no signin'."

"That's no fair." I looked at my father, hoping I could win him over. "Everybody in ma class is goin'."

"Don't be cheeky tae yer mammy an' me."

I backed down, finished my dinner, received a halfpenny for a sweetie from my father and returned to school. All the forms were handed back to Miss McKenzie. Not one was signed.

*

Nessie stayed in Kerr Street where Templeton's carpet factory was. My sister worked there and, on the clear understanding that I would wait at the gate for Madge and come home with her, I was allowed to go to play with Nessie McMillan.

On our way home from school, just before we reached Arcadia Street, where I lived beside Wills Tobacco Factory, Nessie said;

"Away up an tell yer mammy ye're comin' hame wi' me an bring a pencil an paper- we'll get autographs."

"Whit's autographs?"

"People's names."

"Whit people?"

"The Polish sogers. Hurry up."

I ran up the two flights of stairs and told my mother I was going to Nessie's. I took the note pad from my post office set I'd received for my birthday. I somehow knew that I'd better not mention Polish soldiers.

"They're all counts," Nessie informed me.

"Counts?"

"Like kings and princes...cim oan, just haud the paper oot an ask them tae write their names. Wait 'til ye hear them clickin' their heels," she laughed.

*

The soldiers obliged by signing their names in my book. Strange names, and not one clicked his heels. That is, until my sister saw me at the corner of Abercomby Street and London Road. I had stopped two of them and they spoke English. Just as I was about to give one of them my pencil, I felt my shoulder being gripped. I looked up into Madge's face. In my eyes she was lovely and when she wore make-up I thought she was like a film star. So did the Poles.

"Thees ees your sister?"

"Indeed I am." Madge could be very hoity-toity when she spoke.

The young men saluted, clicked their heels, and immediately tried to charm her. One wanted to kiss her hand. She would have none of it.

"Look at zee moon tonight. Ees eet not beautiful like you?"

Madge drew them a look and grabbed my arm.

"Come along and let's get home. Mother will be waiting." To the soldiers, she said,

"Keep your moon talk to yourselves."

"Eet ees a bomber's moon," one of them said, "Be careful, my beautiful meess."

*

My mother sat and knitted at my bedside because I didn't like being in the room by myself. The steady rhythm of her needles soothed away any

fears I had of the dark.

"The French are from France, the Germans are from Germany, the Belgians are from Belgium, the Poles are from Poland," I was telling her.

"Aye, ye're learnin' all right," she smiled.

When she thought I was asleep, she left to join my father in the kitchen.

I waited a while then tiptoed into the lobby and listened at the door. There was maybe a chance she'd changed her mind about me going to America!

"Dick," my mother was saying, "Ah've nearly fifty pounds in the bank. Could we no buy wir son oot o' the army?"

"Not when there's a war oan, Annie. Anyway, ye read his letter. He's being transferred tae the Royal Air Force tae train as a pilot and he's looking forward to it. Cheer up. The War might not be long in finishing. Ah'll make us a cup o' tea. Whit dae ye think o the wean? America indeed!"

My mother laughed.

"Ah think she fancies that everybody in America becomes a film star."

My parents laughed heartily and for some reason I didn't mind them laughing at me.   In fact, I loved the sound.

I looked out of the room window. Wills', the Sheet Metal Works, the Rag Store, the gas lamps. My father had pointed out to me so often that there's nothing there in the dark that's not there in the daylight — there's nothing to be afraid of.

There was no sign of the moon.

My feet were getting cold. I jumped into the bed recess and found my piggy hot-water bottle. I snuggled down. My sister would join me when she came home from the dancing. I always tried to stay awake for my brothers and Madge, but never could. All was well with my world.

The next day a place name which I'd never heard was added to my list.

Clydebank.

A bomber's moon had become a terrible reality.

Phyllis Smart

Travelling with the Corporal

The Corporal arrived at the hospital with a bucket for the dirty napkins, a large newspaper, beetroot sandwiches, and a wet flannel for the baby's bum. We were to catch the 8 am from Euston. Arriving early, for that was the Corporal's way, we boarded a train already packed with troops. This was no gravy train; there were sailors on home-leave, Canadians going to Inveraray on commando training, and Free French joining their unit in Ayr. It seemed most of the armed forces were going to Scotland. I thought of my Scots husband, who was now somewhere in France.

We accepted a courteously offered window seat in a packed carriage and settled down in a Capstan double-strength haze. Our travelling companions were gloriously vulgar at times but always considerate. The newspaper was not required when I breast-fed the baby. The Corporal's thought had been to screen me from lustful glances. There weren't any. The Corporal reckoned it was battle fatigue.

I was not used to babies but the Corporal managed very well, deftly changing the baby and scrutinising for the first signs of nappy rash. A very competent Corporal I was travelling with, always ready with some choice put-down if the banter got out of hand, willing to patrol the platform in Air-Force issue searching out cups of tea, strong enough to scorn offers of help.

We arrived in Glasgow a little after six p.m. with a bucket of crappy napkins and a comatose baby. Only three weeks old, he had been a model on the journey up, either blessed or overcome by Capstan Full Strength.

When we finally arrived in Balloch, we were welcomed in grand style, a red carpet in the lobby and a red flag hanging out the window. My father-in-law was a great supporter of the Russians.

The Corporal stayed for a few days, falling out with my in-laws and warning me that whatever happened I was to stay put. I saw her off on the bus. She was going back to drive the Captain's jeep around London. I felt like saying to hell with the bombs, I'm coming with you, but I'd the wee morsel to worry about and a bucket of napkins.

My intrepid young sister, the Corporal, she should have been directing operations over Normandy or networking her way across Europe. I was very thankful she would get away from driving the Captain.

After the war the Corporal came back to live in Scotland. No longer a Corporal, she trained as a nurse. She was always challenging the system, and focusing on the rights of her patients. Unfettered by doubts, "seize the day" was her maxim.

Today, still a very smart operator, she lives in retirement in Sussex.

Winifred Conway

The Shopping Trip

Quietly, so as not to wake the children, the two women crept up the cellar stair. Ebeth the older girl heard them but she pretended to be asleep.

The war was nearly over and they were trapped at the centre of one of the last battles. In spite of careful rationing the food had finally run out. Ebeth knew her mother had no choice. They will be all right, she told herself. After all, Mother had returned safely every time she had gone to fetch water from the spring.

She watched as her mother took two old canvas bags off the hook on the cellar door and heard her whisper, "Have you got the torch?" "Yes," Maria replied softly and the door closed behind them.

Friederike and Maria climbed the next flight of stairs to the front entrance and tip-toed round the sentry slumped over his machine gun. He jumped up. "Don't worry, I am not asleep," he grinned, but his face was pale and his eyes looked tired.

"Safe return," he said quietly.

"Pray for us," Maria replied. She firmly believed in the power of prayer even if God did not always listen.

The soldier politely opened the front door and the cold blacked-out April night engulfed them.

An earlier explosion had left the garden gate hanging on its bottom hinge. When Friederike tried to move it it crashed down. The noise was deafening.

"Damn", she muttered under her breath, "now we are in for it." They stood frozen, waiting. The rushing sound of the river reminded them that on the other bank the French were ready to attack. Mercifully, all remained quiet.

"God is listening tonight," Maria said.

They picked their way through debris in the road and skirted round the crater in front of the house next door. Old Herr Abrie had been killed there yesterday by a shell. Maria crossed herself. "God rest his soul — he didn't deserve to die like that." Friederike shivered and drew her coat tightly around herself. She thought of her man buried in a cold dark grave in Russia.

"Let's hurry," she said, "I need to get back to my children."

They reached Birkenstrasse. All that was left of the house at number two was a burnt out shell, its blackened chimneystack pointing an accusing finger to the sky.

"Frau Fischer was so proud of her house," Maria sighed, "always buying cleaning materials."

"She will have more time for her children now."

"You have become hard."

"No, not hard, just realistic — I often felt sorry for those boys. Clean, regimented, perfect Hitler Youth material."

They fell silent and walked on towards the dark shadow of the hospital. Only the white outline of the red cross was visible on the sloping roof.

As they passed Professor Eberhardt's garden, the rich scent of wallflowers wafted through the railings. Friederike paused and put her face against the cold iron bars; she was overcome by an aching sense of loss, a yearning for another life that no longer seemed part of her. That contented autumn day, when she, pregnant with her first child, had helped her husband plant a bed of wallflowers. Next spring, he had said, the three of us can sit here and enjoy the perfume of the flowers. She grew vegetables now in her flower garden. Professor Eberhardt had no time for gardening; brought out of retirement, he was now the only surgeon working in the hospital.

Maria put her arms round her friend and led her away. "One day you will grow flowers again," she said.

They reached the end of the road and turned into Bahnhofstrasse, only to be stopped in their tracks. A great mountain of stones and jagged iron barred their way where once the railway bridge had been. They struggled over the rubble and sat down exhausted on the trunk of an uprooted acacia tree. After a few moments Friederike was on her feet again, driven on by the thought of her children alone in the cellar.

"Don't fuss," she said abruptly when she saw Maria examining her broken fingernails and bleeding hands, "Think of the wounded soldiers."

Maria sat motionless. "Wait," she whispered. "Listen, can you hear it?" The lonely drone of a reconnaissance plane circling above struck fear into their hearts. Searchlights criss-crossed the sky showing up grey billowing clouds.

"Please God, don't let them find any bombers."

They sheltered within the tangle of the acacia roots.

"I wish our troops would retreat. If they fight on much longer, we are bound to be bombed," Friederike whispered angrily.

"You know very well they have to obey orders."

"Yes, yes, and our guns are also killing **our** people. Your sister, my sister-in-law and her children over there — they may all be dead by now. We should surrender."

"Hush, keep your voice down", Maria implored her. "What would people say if they heard you?"

"Oh Maria, why don't you accept it — we are beaten. All I am fighting for now is my children."

Friederike bent down and picked up the bags. "Let's go now, we have to be off the streets before daybreak."

*

Maria's shop stood in the 'better' part of the town. Before the war she was proud to satisfy her customer's demands for the best of everything. Parma ham, caviar from Russia, cheeses and paté de foie gras from France. Whatever they asked for — Maria was happy to supply.

She was tolerant of their snobbish little ways and obliged when they insisted on being addressed by their husband's titles; Frau Professor Eberhardt, Frau Director Biedermann, Frau Doctor Muenzenmaier. When it was rumoured that some of her customers obtained luxury goods and even coffee on the Black Market, Maria would have none of it — her ladies were above suspicion.

As they turned in to the yard at the back of the shop, Maria reached for her key. She didn't need it — the door was wide open. Smashed. Shadowy figures were moving about, dragging crates and sacks. She heard the sound of breaking glass and angry quarrelling voices, which she recognised only too well. At that moment Maria's faith in humanity collapsed. She sat down on the cold cobblestones and wept.

Friederike resolutely marched through the broken doorway and filled her bags.

Elisabeth Fry

Baltic Encounter

The newsreader announced that British and French troops had that day been sent into Egypt to secure the Suez Canal. The Russian Ambassador to the United Nations had been making serious threats about the consequences. He was clearly indicating that military action was being considered.

The ship was loading the final consignment of deck cargo in the Swedish port of Ornskoldsvik, in the Gulf of Bothnia. Telegraph poles, deeply impregnated with creosote, were piled high on deck. They were highly inflammable, and the dockers were securing them against any movement on the voyage.

"Second Mate," said the Captain, "I don't like the sound of this. The Russian Fleet'll be loose in the Baltic, right across our route south. No bloody Ruskie is going to get my ship — I'll burn her first! Go you ashore to the Agent, and get ten 5-gallon drums of petrol. I want them aboard before we sail tonight."

The ship sailed, with two drums of petrol carefully secured among the deck cargo at each of the five hatches. Next day things in Suez were not going well, and the Russian threat was savagely real. The news spread through the ship quickly, and the lifeboat drill, which was usually fairly perfunctory, was done with great seriousness. Many of the crew were war survivors, and knew the horrors of sinking. After passing through the Alland Islands into the Baltic, the lifeboats were swung out to emergency position, and everyone put on alert. Would the Russians attack a lone British Merchantman in such confined waters? Few doubted that there was that possibility. What could be done if they did? Better to be prepared. It was not a comfortable feeling.

The sea was calm. Darkness was beginning to fall. It was about 10.00 pm, when the Third Mate saw three ships, hull-down to port. A quick look through the glasses identified them as warships, but in the gathering gloom he could not make out any flag. The Captain came on the bridge to see for himself. "Aye they'll have us on radar. About ten miles, I would say. What do you think, Third?"

"Aye Captain, just in shelling range."

"You're right about that, but we will just have to hope that they ignore us. I'm going down to see the Mate and the Chief. Keep me informed if there is any change."

Midnight came and the warships were still on station. The Radio Operator reported that there did not seem to be any significant increase in traffic on the air. It had become heavily overcast and very dark, and the lights of the other ships could be seen only occasionally. The Second Mate was taking bearings from shore lights some 15 miles off, and Sparks was dozing quietly in the radio room. It was 2.20 am when the lookout called out, "A blue light low in the water, two points on the port bow!" A submarine!!! There was no need to call the Captain, for he was up on the bridge ladder, three at a time. "Call all hands. Put the engines on standby. Stand by the petrol drums. Get all other crew to lifeboat stations." It was like wartime all over again.

"Can you still see him, Second?"

"Aye Captain, he's closing on us." The Crew were tumbling out of the accommodation, pulling on lifejackets and cursing their luck to be called out.

Suddenly the darkness was split by a blindingly white light coming from the submarine. Morse Code - Di Dah Di Dah. "Christ, he's calling us! Answer him Second, but try to stall him!"

The Second Mate sent back the standard reply, "I am receiving you — proceed .."

"What ship and where bound?"

"Do you think we should tell him?" said the Captain.

"What if they're neutral... A Swede?"

"No, just answer him, but take your time!"

"S.S. Rora bound from Ornskoldsvik to Southampton," spelled out the Aldis lamp, as slowly as possible. "Received," came the reply, then darkness. "He's looking up our Registry," said the Captain, "to see if we're the Enemy! Sparks, see if there's radio traffic now. Is he calling up the surface ships?"

"Captain, there's something calling very close, possibly him, but it's in a military code. I can't make it out."

"Damn! Ask him who he is, Second."

"What ship?" sent the Second.

The few seconds' pause seemed like eternity to those standing on the bridge. Then the reply came, quite slowly, almost as if the submarine was teasing them.

"Swedish warships on patrol. Bon Voyage."

Jack Paul

From Under the Counter

With a nod and a wink and an air of conferring something special, the butcher reached under the counter, lifted out a large parcel, and laid it in my shopping basket.

"A wee treat for you," he said. My legitimate ration of a half pound of mince lay on top of the parcel, shamed into insignificance.

At this stage of the war treats were, like everything else, in very short supply. I wondered what gastronomic delight was in store, and hurried home to find out. When I unwrapped the parcel, I was horrified. On the table lay a sheep's head; the actual skull of a dead sheep. It had been scraped clean of flesh, it had great gaping holes where the eyesockets had been but it still had a full set of teeth. Cocooned in its nest of paper, it lay and grinned at me. A good soup bone was hard to come by. This one was almost worth its weight in gold. I knew I should be grateful, but ......

It was the teeth that put me off. Judging by the teeth, it must have been a healthy animal. It had a complete set, large, strong and yellow, edged with black where the gums had been. It fixed me with that ghastly grin, and I shuddered as we studied each other. I tried to motivate myself with the thought of the transformation that long, slow boiling and the addition of vegetables, peas and barley would make. There would be enough good nourishing soup for two days, perhaps more. A treat indeed! But first, something would have to be done about the teeth. I wondered if bleach would affect the taste of the soup. No! Better not risk it.

It would have to be the scrubbing brush. It didn't bear thinking about. Perhaps I should just toss the monstrosity away and say nothing about it. Yes! Who would know? I rewrapped it tightly and threw it into the dustbin. Two minutes later, my conscience fished it out again. Tomorrow's another day, I told myself, I'll deal with it tomorrow. (I had recently seen Gone With The Wind.)

That night was my night out. Each week my friend and I went to the pictures, while our husbands babysat. Our shillingsworth of escapism, they called it. It failed to work that night. The image of the grinning skull insistently superimposed itself between me and Clark Gable. It would not be banished. It even followed me home — "preceded me" would be more accurate — because it bobbed along about a yard in front of my face in a travesty of a lonely Scottish reel. It had acquired an eerie greenish glow, which lit up the blackout around it. I expected each moment to hear the familiar shout from the Air Raid Warden of "Put out that light."

When I reached home, the real sheep's head still lay on the table, but beside it there now lay a pair of pliers. It was a shadow of its former self, for it no longer grinned at me. My husband had pulled out every single tooth. It was no longer an object of menace; it was simply the makings of a pot of broth. It looked pathetic. I almost, but not quite, felt sorry for it. I never asked what had become of the teeth.

The following evening my family voted the soup the best they had had for a long time. I wouldn't know. I didn't have any.

Elizabeth MacLean

War's Reality

This was the time of war with Nazi Germany. I knew enough from my politically aware parents that this was serious. I'd knitted squares for blankets, to help the Spanish people fighting for their country against Fascism. I'd met children from Spain and Austria, who had fled from wars that had engulfed their families. But so far I was untouched, and, apart from carrying my gas mask, found it unreal.

Unreal until the day I found myself walking on the Downs with a small group of Woodcraft Folk members. It was autumn. The sun shone from a clear blue sky, and the blackberries were ripe. We were young, strong, innocent, and without fear.

We stopped to eat our sandwiches, sitting on the side of a hill overlooking a valley which went down to the English Channel. The peace seemed infinite. Suddenly someone said "There's a big lorry, down there". We all looked down, and saw not a lorry, but a German plane zigzagging up the valley. The Iron Cross was clear on the side of its grey body. We were transfixed, motionless. I swear none of us could breathe. As it went out of sight, we hurled ourselves down to the shelter of a belt of trees, shaken and unable to put our feelings into words.

Later we returned to our abandoned sandwiches, which we could not eat, and so made our way home, subdued and thoughtful.

Sheila Rees

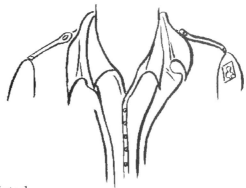

Regimental Ties

The tie sparked
memories they didn't know existed.
Red stripes on navy blue,
a sign of engineers and gentlemen,
the regiment.

Remember when we basked
under an Egyptian sun
guarding the POWs?
Knowing escape across the desert
was not an option contemplated
by other than a fool.

An easy camp, where enmity
back-seated.
Those poor devils
hadn't orchestrated war.
Our house still boasts
a table artisaned by one
whose bayonet was grounded.

They were just men who lost
And we, victorious,
were losers, too.
So many yarns ago ....
Yet ties still knot.

Pamela Duncan

Winds Blow Cold

winds blow cold
scars ache
long after wounds are healed
old soldiers remember

Pat Irvine

When Blood is Nipp'd

Winter set in early that year of 1935; after a long summer there was almost no autumn. The harshness of the wintry conditions, and the onset of long hours of darkness, brought home to Jean the reality of her situation - and a yearning for home.

Although tearful as her mother and brother left without her at the end of their summer holiday, a sense of adventure had made the parting bearable. In any case she had little say in the matter. There would be one less mouth to feed back in Glasgow, where there was only 'short-time' work for her father. Poor though her grandmother was, she was considered better-off than those living in the city. She had a meagre pension, but also a cow, hens, and some sheep.

The first weeks at the new school proved difficult. There was the long three-mile walk twice daily. The other scholars were native Gaelic speakers, who mocked Jean's Glasgow accent. Bespectacled and shy, as well as small for her age, she suffered in silence until her curiosity value diminished. She missed the orderliness of the segregated playgrounds of her old school. She found the boys too boisterous. The freedom to roam outwith school grounds came as a surprise.

Her granny's way of fortifying her for the colder weather was to provide more brose in the mornings. A parcel from home was found to contain a pair of black leather calf-length boots. Jean had never worn boots before, and hated them on sight. Granny reinforced the soles and heels with tackets. She prayed for rain when she would be allowed to wear wellingtons, but instead there was frost covering the landscape, and ice on the lochs.

Communication between Jean and her grandmother was a problem at times, for the old lady spoke very little English and the girl, while understanding Gaelic, was reluctant to speak it. Her granny had never learned to read and write because, as the eldest girl in a large family, she had not often been sent to school on the remote island where she had been born. It was strange that she could read her Bible, from which she took great comfort, and they had worship morning and evening.

The icy conditions could not keep that religious community from attending church, so old and young walked each Sabbath to one or other of the three churches. Jean found the Gaelic services long, and understood little of what was being preached. The singing seemed tuneless and mournful. There were mid-week prayer meetings too, held in houses in different villages each week.

Attendance at the prayer meetings were almost their only outings in the evenings. Walking on dark nights, with only a hurricane lamp to guide their steps, made Jean shiver with a mixture of fear and excitement, as she clung to her grandmother's coat-tails. She was afraid of the dark. On moonlit nights, her imagination would run riot as shadows formed into strange and eerie shapes on the hills and moorland.

It was snug in the wee house when the door was shut, after the hens had been locked in, and the cow milked in the byre. A peat fire burning in the old grate, the paraffin lamp lit, the clicking of her granny's knitting needles, and the purring of the cat (nameless) made Jean feel warm and secure. The cat was not intended as a pet, and was put out after worship, before they went to bed.

There was another familiar smell most evenings, as granny rubbed Sloan's Liniment into her granddaughter's feet, which were red and sore with chilblains.

It was during that winter that granny learned to write the alphabet, copying out the letters very laboriously. It was a proud old lady who was finally able to sign her pension book 'Catherine Gillanders', instead of making an 'X'.

Jean MacBeath

Country
Memories

How well I remember my childhood. I grew up on a farm in South Lanarkshire, three miles from the nearest village and six miles from the nearest small town. There were no school buses, and the long walk to school meant leaving home quite early in the morning. My mother, a stickler for punctuality, packed me off each morning in plenty of time to arrive long before school started. I was always first through the school gates, although I never hurried.

I found that every season had a magic of its own. In Spring, the hedges of beech and hawthorn were full of the sounds of birds building their nests. I became quite an expert at recognising the different eggs in the nests. Blackbirds, sparrows, thrushes and finches were the most common, but sometimes I would find a robin's nest. Lambs were appearing in the fields and I would spend ages leaning on the fence watching them running and jumping, just full of life.

If the weather was wet or stormy, my father would take me to school on the bar of his bicycle, sheltered from the elements by his waterproof cape. As soon as I was old enough to ride a bicycle, I would cycle to and from school by myself. Of course the roads were quite quiet in those days, and sometimes I wouldn't meet anyone at all until I reached the village.

Summer was wonderful too with the grass verges and hedgerows full of wild flowers - daisies, buttercups, harebells, vetches, cuckoo pint, ragged robin and tiny blue speedwell (or "cat's eyes" as they were commonly called). The banks of the burn were bright with masses of yellow marsh marigolds. When hay-making time came round, I liked to see the hay being cut and dried and built into ricks, then loaded on to the ricklifter and pulled by a sturdy Clydesdale back to the farm to be built into one large haystack which then had to be covered by a tarpaulin. My cousins and I thoroughly enjoyed rides on the ricklifter.

Often, during the school holidays, my grandfather would take me with him to Lanark market, travelling by special bus which ran every Market Day from Leadhills to Lanark, picking up farmers, and sometimes their wives, at the farm road-ends all along the way. This was always a special treat for me, as I loved the atmosphere of the Market. It was exciting listening to the auctioneer who spoke so fast I could scarcely follow him. I was careful to sit very still and not scratch my nose or put a hand up to smooth my hair in case I became the owner of a prize bull or a flock of sheep!

Another exciting event in the farming calendar was the threshing of the corn once the harvest was safely gathered in. This was long before the advent of combine harvesters and mechanised farming. The threshing machine, or "big mill" as it was commonly known, visited the farms in turn. Each farmer helped his neighbour at the big mill by sending one or two of his workers. Threshing was a really hard job, forking the heavy sheaves of corn to keep the mill busy. It was also extremely noisy and while threshing was in progress conversation was virtually impossible. One had to shout loudly to have any chance of being heard above the clatter of the machine. It was also an unpleasant job, with dust and chaff flying around getting up the noses and into the throats and eyes of the workers.

An added hazard was the large number of field mice that fled from the sheaves of corn and raced around in a panic. Most workers tied string round their trouser legs to prevent the unhappy experience of a mouse finding refuge there. As there were often women working at the threshing, you can imagine the shrieks of terror at such an occurrence! Of course, the farm cats had a field day.

Around mid-day there would be a rest period during which the farmer's wife would bring out refreshments which consisted of tea and jam sandwiches, or "jeely pieces" which were very welcome. The break over, it was back to work once more until the threshing was finally finished. Then everyone would troop wearily into the farm kitchen where a hearty meal awaited them. The farmer's wife would usually have been busy baking girdle scones and pancakes, which soon vanished like the proverbial "snow off a dyke." Of course there was also an unlimited supply of good strong tea, though no doubt many of the men would be calling in to the local hotel to slake their thirst with a pint or two on their way home.

Netta Jess

The Village Blacksmith

One of my earliest memories is of waking in my grandparents' house with the sun streaming in at the window, and the ringing sound of hammer on anvil from the smiddy next door. I loved that smiddy, where my grandfather and father worked along with a hired man called Geordie. My grandfather was a Boer War veteran, having been a farrier with a cavalry regiment.

A few pulls on the bellows would bring the seemingly dead fire in the forge into glowing life, so that strips of iron could be made red hot and hammered into the shape of a horse's hoof. Each time the hammer made contact, the "smiddy sparks" would fly upwards. To a child's eyes this was something quite magical. The making of the groove for the nail came next. It required two men to make these holes, seven in every shoe. One would hold a sharp pointed hammer in position while the other, with the swing of a heavy mallet, would drive the point straight through.

When the horse's old shoes had been removed, the hooves were cleaned and pared. The new shoe was fitted against the hoof while it was still very hot. This burned a groove, into which the shoe would be finally placed. Any adjustments necessary were made at this stage. The shoe was then cooled by plunging it into a bucket of cold water. The nailing on of the shoe had to be done very carefully, the points of the nails coming to the outside of the hoof. The points were then filed off, and the hooves brushed with oil. A wet day during harvest time would bring a rush of business, and there would be a queue of horsemen each with his pair. It would stretch all the way up the lane and spill onto the street.

A few years ago while on holiday, I saw an itinerant blacksmith arrive at the riding stables. In his van he carried shoes of various sizes and fitted and nailed them on cold. I wondered how long they would stay in place.

Betty Jack

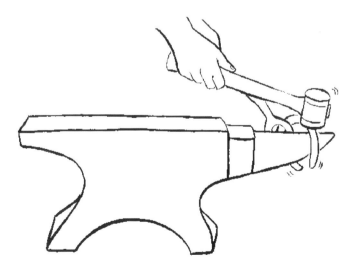

Horniegoloch   *

I pou'd a brierbud
frae a drookit bush;
oot rin a horniegoloch,
Euch!
It fairly scunnert me tae look .

Ye're no' a bonny thing at a'
Yer body's nearly black
an a'... like ... cleekit doon the back,
tae mak ye scutter roon aboot
wi' thae queer crescent horns,
ye arenae braw tae see.

But syne, wee goloch,
keekin up at me,
ye'll shairly spy a maist byordinar beast,
an' weel ye micht remark,
"Yon peely-wally, hornless cratur
cannae be the guid God's wark."

* earwig

Pat Irvine

The Booth

The fat woman sat looking out at the rain as it lashed across the streaming timbers, merging with the spray being hurled in incandescent sheets over the railings. The two seemed to be dancing together, skittering over the glistening black pools of water that now covered the walkway. A sudden wild gust tore past and she watched as it ripped the front facing off the Punch and Judy stall. The dirty heavy canvas banged and flapped in the whistling wind, giving the empty stall an almost eerie look, the only sound to be heard through the weather on this silent, slate-grey day. It seemed to be beating out a message. She knew he wouldn't come today. Not with this rain. He always had a cold and usually a drip at the end of his nose. No, the Punch and Judy man would not come today!

The bright purple and yellow ochre that was the fat woman wrapped her floating garments more closely around her and warmed her fingerless gloved hands at the little gas ring. She boiled the blackened tin kettle, dropped in a tea bag and sweetener, then spooned a heaped teaspoonful of thick, white condensed milk into the old cracked mug. Licking the spoon like a deprived cat, she burrowed deep below her many layers and produced a well worn leather hip flask. A stream of crystal clear gin whirlpooled its way through the dense creamy layer. She lifted the ancient mug in both hands, swallowed deeply and allowed her thoughts to wander off to the brightly coloured walls surrounding her.

Old frayed circus posters, photographs of trapeze artists, lion tamers, acrobats, clowns formed a mighty collage on the three walls. Torn corners peeked through behind more recent theatre programmes and yellowed newspaper cuttings, pinned, sellotaped and stuck down, then re-stuck a hundred times over. It had all begun back there, back in the days when, bareback, she had ridden with great grace and daring around that mighty sawdust ring. She could almost smell it still - the warm tang of the animals, the sharp scent of urine in the damp sawdust, the sweet oils of the trapezists, the sweat and sexual excitement of the performers - a glorious wonderful world of sights, smells and brilliant colours. And now she was here. A rather fat ridiculous relic of glamorous days long gone. Her eyes still sparkled, her laugh was loud and clean and even if she wobbled and bounced a bit when she walked, she still enjoyed regaling some patient visitor with tales of ENSELIA, a beautiful bareback rider. Sometimes she would hear faint tittering as some of them walked out of sight, but others were genuinely intrigued and interested.

The day wore on and not a soul appeared, not even the ice cream vendor, none of the fancy hats and balloon people or the hot whelks man.

She looked at her neat rolls of tickets - blue for entry, adults 30p., children 15p., yellow for the roundabout, red for the Punch and Judy Man. She had missed the chat about the old days they always had as she brewed him a cup after each show. She would buy some tickets, keep them in her drawer and say that people had come and booked for the following day. That might cheer him up and make him feel he was still the star turn.

She fought the squalling wind as she battened down the boards of the booth, checked the makeshift lacing she had patched into the torn canvas of the Punch and Judy stall and looked around quickly through the driving rain. The lights of the trams on the sea front were like flickering candles beckoning her to their cosy, familiar leather seats. She fastened the big billowing yellow oilskin cape, put her red raffia basket over her arm and headed off down the deserted pier. She would take a tram ride before she went home to her room, maybe stop off first at the public house on the corner for a glass of stout. There would be someone there she could talk to and tell about her day on the pier.

Tomorrow her friend would be back, the sun would come out and with it the pier people. The visitors would tramp noisily down the springing planks of the boardwalk and she would look out some new posters for her booth. Feeling reassured, she stepped happily into the welcoming warmth of the waiting tram. Yes! Tomorrow would be a good day in Enselia's booth.

Heather Bruyere Watt

Rottenrow *
in the
Sixties

The labour room, aptly named, was similar to a public lavatory; large white tiles, grouting grey cement, stone floor, all very easy to slunge down. There were screens between each bed but no real privacy. The shouting could be colourful. "I want my Mammy, O God, help me, help me!" No mention of Dads. They had enjoyed the conception but birth was no part of their remit.

To a new trainee inexperienced midwife it looked like a torture chamber, or a scene from Dante's Inferno. Large sterilisers steamed away merrily day and night, and autoclaves for the various instruments (especially the large forceps) would have looked more in keeping in an abattoir.

The first delivery witnessed was equally horrendous. Some pale nameless woman was having her baby pulled out by the use of these instruments. The obstetrician was sweating, pulling and tugging.

Eventually to our amazement a live baby was produced. The tutor took us back to the classroom and admitted on reflection that this had not been the best introduction to the labour ward.

Individual women stay in your memory. Jessie signed herself out to go home to a derelict house on Monteith Row with a shared cooker on the landing. My instructions were to change the baby out of hospital clothes and bring the mother's dressing gown and blanket back. There were no baby clothes and no blankets so I just left them, wondering at her predicament and realising what the term 'born to fail' meant.

In contrast, home delivery could be peaceful and quiet, with all the family present and the midwife fitting in as a member of that close- knit unit. But there was no sense in being lulled into a feeling of false security. The home could be extremely poor, with only a shared toilet on the stair, and no proper kitchen facilities. For a woman who had too many children there was the added risk of haemorrhage, as well as the worry of wee children getting up in the night to use the potty and wondering what was going on. For the midwife, there was the awesome responsibility for a new life and a mother's wellbeing, and the joy and relief when the baby gasped and cried. A miracle.

There were wonderful midwives but thank goodness for the flying squad.

We felt extremely proud to be wearing our uniform of navy coat and a small black straw hat with bows that tied under our chin. We travelled all over Glasgow and our constant companion was the Glasgow Corporation bus time-table. We were experts in the geography of the city. It was a privilege and pleasure to be of service to these indomitable women.

* Glasgow Royal Maternity Hospital

Ercell Carruthers

Old Tenement

Cold hissing greenish
gaslight makes long-legged shadows
on paintless walls

where stone stairs spiral
into echoing darkness.
Brass doorbells are dumb.

Pat Irvine

Vanmen
Calling

My boyhood memories are associated with the various vanmen that called in the village. Each vanman had his own particular morning afternoon or evening for calling, and it was an absolute delight to hear them calling out their respective goods. Their voices, on occasions helped by a shrill blast on a whistle, echoed through the village streets with such sounds as this;

"B-a-y-k-u-r".... The word was stretched out, with the emphasis on the first syllable, and was immediately followed by a shrill blast on a whistle. All of this was repeated several times. "B-o-o-c-h-u-r"... was performed in much the same manner. However one vanman shortened his version and it came out like "c-h-e-r-r".... Short and sharp!

The fruiterer vans that called in the village presented their vanmen with a problem. Their trade name came out like "t-e-r-e-r".... the first part being lost entirely. However, not to be outsmarted, they improvised, and would quickly add 'delicious mackintosh reds" or 'pearsnplums" or "jaffa owranges," to great sales effect.

I can't remember whether Jock Millar the coalman called out his merchandise by name or not. He probably didn't need to, as his customers always heard the clip-clop-clip-clop of his horses' hooves. What I do remember is the arrival of the trader in briquettes, who called "B-r-e-e-a-k-e-t-s." Sometimes it was stretched out to "B-r-e-e-a-k-e-t-s" followed by the Stanley Baxter type Glesgaranto expression, "Dizzenfurrabobe."...He could be heard all over the village, and so could all the other vanmen. Sssh! Can you hear them calling now?

Another vanman I remember came every Saturday without fail. He came in a wee white van, and he quickly began advertising his products by calling out loud and clear, short and sharp; "Ribs! Ribs! Ribs! Lovely pork ribs! Ribs! Ribs! Ribs!" I think he came from somewhere in Ayrshire, either Darvel or Galston. He sold lovely pork and ham ribs, and when served up piping hot they were absolutely delicious. I can always remember hoping that my mother would be one of his Saturday morning customers, for this was a mid-day treat not to be missed.

And I almost forgot about the ragmen. Their call went something like this, "D-e-l-f-u-r-r-a-g-s....d-e-l-f-u-r-r-a-g-s," or sometimes, "b-a-l-l-o-o-n-f-u-r-r-a-g-s," to attract younger customers. I imagine "delf" referred to the plain cups and saucers, sometimes plates, they exchanged with mothers for bags of old rags or unwanted clothes. "Delfurrags! Delfurrags!" The call of "Delfurrags" was always followed by a terrific blast from an old battered army bugle that went echoing round the streets. Can you hear it?

Iain Turner

Odd
Bods

Did you wear a liberty-bodice when you were young? I did.

A strange name for an even stranger garment, it went on over a vest and buttoned down the front. It had vertical tapes sewn on at regular intervals, and more buttons round the bottom; linen, as I recall, not to break in the mangle. It was like a mini-corset without bones, and was worn only in winter.

My friend Anne had something quite different. She wore hand-knitted undies, courtesy of her granny, who lived with them. She and her younger sister were considered 'delicate' and from October onwards were swaddled in a knitted set of vest and pants, plus a knitted pair of combinations, topped off with woollen stockings, jumpers and cardigans. Between the first two layers, they sported a thick layer of Thermogene, a sort of yellow cotton wool, known as a chest protector. As war-time wool was anything but kind to the skin, they must have suffered severe discomfort, and alas, they seemed to suffer from continual sniffles, despite the family's effort to keep them healthy. In my teens, suspenders were buttoned onto my bodice and these supported a most refined form of torture - long woollen stockings.

How well I remember the service which was held in the Assembly Hall in school every Monday morning. As I stood there the itch would start, usually during a prayer, and I would frantically rub my legs together, as scratching would have been unthinkable, but it didn't help at all. Later I graduated to lisle stockings which were much more bearable.

At the first blink of spring sunshine, I would beg my mother to be rid of these encumbrances, but she would refuse, triumphantly pointing out certain acquaintances, all ankle-sock wearers, whose hideously mottled legs told their own story of sitting too close to the fire on winter evenings.

"You'll thank me for it when you're older," she would say.

It was always a happy day when finally I was allowed to discard them. And I shall never forget the wonderful feeling of freedom that was mine, the day the liberty-bodice went back into the drawer for the summer.

Nada Mooney

Sunday, Sunday

Sunday is the worst day of the week.

I attend church wearing my best, which are too big on account of my mother buying them roomy so's I can grow into them. My Sunday shoes blister my heels. I complain, and my mother tells me I'm ungrateful, and to think of the poor starving orphans with no shoes and only rags to wear. Thinking of barefoot raggedy orphans sure don't help stinging blisters.

Before we leave for church my mother recites her don't list, which gets longer every week. Today she adds yawning to the regular fidgeting, scratching, coughing, giggling and gawping. Then she tells me three times not to make her ashamed of me.

My father doesn't go to church, because he isn't a hypocrite. He stays at home and thinks beautiful thoughts.

Of all the people who come to church there are some we don't sit beside. Mr Fitzroy drinks the best Irish stout on a Saturday night so we sit as far as possible from him. Miss Flora Stoddart has decayed teeth and bad breath so we don't sit in front of her. Miss Matilda, the bank manager's daughter, makes her own hats the size of cartwheels. We don't sit behind her. We don't sit near the Finkles either. Mr Finkle sleeps through the service. Sometimes he snores and sounds like he's throwing marbles in an enamel pail. It's hard to believe so much noise could come from such a small, skinny man. Everyone calls him Mr Rip Van. His wife is a very large lady with a big bust. We also don't sit under the leak in the roof.

The sermon is always about eternal life and eternal damnation. The preacher has a don't list longer than my mother's. After ten minutes his face gets red, his voice becomes louder, and he thumps the pulpit so hard he wakens Mr Rip Van. He stares at me when he talks about the sinners who are damned. Just when I think he has said it all he starts again. That's when my scalp starts to itch, just a little at first. It feels like two spiders chasing each other. They breed and hundreds of them run all over my head. I scratch and claw. My mother kicks me on the ankle. A spider falls down the back of my neck and I start to squirm. She nips my thigh. I lean back against the pew as hard as I can and squash the spider.

A tickle starts at the back of my throat. I'll die if I don't cough. As gently and quietly as I can, I cough. It sounds like a trumpet. Why does the preacher stop talking just then? The congregation takes it as a signal for mass coughing. The preacher glares at me again. If he's got anything to do with it I'm never going to get to heaven.

Pregnant ladies faint in church - that's how everyone knows they are pregnant. Today Mrs Rip Van fainted and she fell right on top of poor Mr Rip Van who was dozing peacefully. It took six people to lift her. I don't think she's pregnant. She just sat next to Mr Fitzroy.

After the service the Reverend stands by the door and shakes hands with the congregation as they leave, and they tell him how consoling and uplifting his sermon was. When he can't hear, they call him an old windbag who says the same thing every week. If you ask me, when I grow up I'll be a non-hypocrite, and stay at home on Sunday, and just think.

Or maybe by then we will have a new preacher.

Margaret Morgan

Good Memories for Bad Days

Mother 'phoned late on a wet miserable Saturday. Something was wrong. Father was on the floor, he couldn't get up. He was on all fours, knees and elbows resting on the carpet. She thought he looked quite ridiculous, like a dog who wanted to wag its tail but had lost it somewhere. Kneeling beside him she said as much; then she saw the twisted mouth. And the fear in his eyes. Stroke. The word roared through her brain.

Nervous fingers prodded the telephone. "I need the doctor. It's an emergency."

He came at last, in black tie and dinner suit. But he came. "Sorry," he said, "Not a lot of hope – if he survives the night – well – who knows."

Night or day he was never left alone. She lifted, shifted, washed and changed him. She dripped water and clear soup from a teaspoon between his distorted lips then started all over again. Minute helpings of strained baby food and sloppy yoghurt were coaxed down while she explained what had happened without really understanding herself.

Later, when his chest crackled and croaked, she thumped up globs of disgusting phlegm persistently filling his lungs. One week and a day after he didn't die, pneumonia got him the hospital bed where he fought and wept throughout the next months until he could stand and drag his feet a few paces. And then he went home.

He wasn't back long when she discovered that attempting to crawl through the locked cells in a damaged brain could be as nerve-wracking as inching through a war zone, and could just as easily end in disaster. However, when the elusive laughter button was somehow touched, all the effort was worthwhile, even when events under discussion were dismissed with an angry flourish of his walking stick. The frustration caused by his poor speech meant that getting it wrong could be downright dangerous, so Mother learned, albeit the hard way, to tread common ground. Or in their case, water.

From the first raft he built as a child to the Russian Convoys during the second World War, the sea was in his veins, in spite of the fact that the raft sank like a stone and a couple of the naval cruisers he served on ended up as multistorey fish parks for marine life on route to Murmansk. But after the war his real joy was his very own pride of the Clyde, a lifeboat he rescued from the breaker's yard and converted to a cabin cruiser.

When she teased him about the scrapes they had gotten into on the 'high seas', a faraway glint would flicker deep in his rheumy eyes. On more than one occasion she was poked by the dreaded stick while rattling out vague memories of daring deeds best forgotten.

"Don't you — " he'd splutter, "Don't you — wheesht!" Maybe his speech was not so good, but there was nothing wrong with his aim.

"We were lucky," she once said to him. "We escaped from Glasgow during the summer. Remember how we used to head up the Kyles? What was the name of thon wee beach?"

"Don't know – fost – frost – forst – You know!"

"Got it!" she shouted out , then blushed furiously at the stupidity of her mouth.

"Right! You called it Forestwaters! Couldn't think for a minute there."

His shoulders jiggled up and down. He was laughing for the first time in weeks and it didn't matter if it was at her embarrassment.

"Wheel," he said, his good hand moving in a circle. "Wheel – dum – dum – humpity – You know!" The frustration of not joining up the right words always ended in 'you know.'

At that moment she didn't know. Having buried the dread of blood and bandages, her mind had jumped to matching colours on a plastic strip after lancing one of his fingers. Then she remembered. There was doubtful relief in her tone when she spoke. "You mean our engine song?"

But had she put the clues together properly? The wheelhouse was where the engine was. "Dum-dum" had to be some sort of a tune and of course the 'humpity' had been a sound peculiar to their old Albion bus engine when it was running sweet. Suddenly he grinned and she reckoned her guess had been good. She started singing their own special 'sea shanty' of almost forty years ago and the look on his face said Pavarotti couldn't have done it better.

Her mind flitted back through the years to when this shrunken figure answered every question she had ever needed to ask. To the days when the two of them used to prowl deserted beaches and woods hunting for treasure, buried or otherwise. The wealth they unearthed came only in odd shaped bottles washed in on the tide although sometimes they might see a colony of seals sunning on a rock or catch a glimpse of speckled birds' eggs nestling in sand and reeds.

A cold finger of regret touched her conscience. Tomorrow she would try to organise some time to push him down to the loch to see the boats. Maybe some talk of past beachcoming episodes would help them battle through the first hours of a new day.

Ellen Lamont

Black and White

At midnight, when the others skipped off to the hotel nightclub, my daughter Anna joined them. Nobody goes to bed on a White Night, I was told. It is impossible to sleep. I had found that true.

Since my arrival in Leningrad several nights before, I had wandered the corridors, got into conversation with the Floor Lady, and had engaged in a debate about the Great Patriotic War with an American, who informed me he had been a lecturer at Strathclyde University. Because I belonged to Glasgow, he assured me, I could butt in. I declined. Both her grating rasp and his nasal twang sent me back to sleeplessness in St. Petersburg.

Where was the magic in these White Nights? I wasn't going to seek it out. I had a nightcap from the Berioska shop and a good book to see me through the night everyone wanted to turn into day.

The book and bottle failed to put me to sleep. My face was pressed against the window at 3.00 am. A procession of people paraded up and down. Big women in headscarves, and bearded Rasputins in jeans made the street as busy as Nevsky Prospect, with its purposeful crowds. But where were they all going at this time of night? (Or should it be morning?) No use me taking a walk to cure my insomnia. Yesterday afternoon I had been approached by a polite youth who asked if I had anything at all to sell. Then an old man had asked in English, straight from a phrase book, which land had I journeyed from. He was at pains to ensure I would not consider him impolite. Faced with his gestures and bows of appeasement, how could I? He belonged to another era.

I waited in vain for darkness. In the curious eerie light, I noticed lengths of fur hanging from a pulley outside the windows of flats opposite. I wondered where this city dweller had trapped his prize sables, if that's what they were. I returned to my book which told me that the twenty-fifth of May starts the White Nights, when night never comes and evening twilight melts into dawn; that White Nights are the 'whitest' from June 11th to July 2nd; that they end around July 20th.

I must have dozed some, drifted some, my thoughts haunted by Russian monster breakfasts of fried potatoes topped with sour cream, four-course affairs, everything awash with sour cream.

I'll never forget my last breakfast in Russia. These were pre-glasnost days, and everyone was anxious to impress Westerners. Each one of the four courses included a heap of caviar. It was indeed a black start to the day. Perhaps some people acquired a taste for it. Maybe I'm just not a morning person.

Helen McLuckie

Culture
Shock

Nothing can prepare a Westerner going to work in Japan for those first few weeks. You think at first, they're just like us, really. You're surprised to find what seem to be only superficial differences. There are elegant department stores, streamlined trains, efficient buses, (perhaps not so like us after all), and traffic drives on the left. The advertisements are strange and exotic, but the names are familiar; Sony, Nissan, Hitachi. Very soon doubts arise.

For a start, there were the gifts. Our President welcomed me in a short but formal ceremony, and presented me with a clock. I thought, I wonder what you get when you leave. In the first few weeks, there was a torrent of gifts from everyone I came in contact with. All kinds of things were given; tea sets, towels, and kitchen equipment, like the shower parties we used to have for engagements and new babies. It was all rather embarrassing, until I found out the Japanese philosophy of gift-giving. Duty or obligation is central to their culture. One must never be in someone's debt, and the only way to avoid this is to give a reciprocal gift or service. So in Japan, (and people would tell me this utterly without guile), if you give a gift you can then expect a favour. They now have a credit with you, and some day they'll ask for the pay-off. Everyone knows the system, and they're only surprised that Westerners don't see how neat it is.

There are rules governing all aspects of living. I knew about bowing, but hadn't realised that there is a prescribed depth of bow for each encounter, which depends on age, sex, professional status, length of acquaintance and a few other subtleties. Too low a bow is just as socially offensive as not bowing low enough. Unfortunately, Japanese politeness forbids them to correct you, which would be insulting, so they can be curling up inside at such crassness, while still smiling benignly. I suspect the only way they cope is to make allowances for us foreign barbarians. It is also unacceptable to address anyone, or even refer to them, without adding the honorific "-san" to their name. And it's impolite to offer an opinion on anything more controversial than food or the weather; this tends to kill conversation stone dead for a Westerner. In fact, though I met with nothing but kindness and consideration during my time there, I was always on edge in case I offended, and constantly waited to see how they did it before responding.

I really began to get a glimmer of what lay ahead during a meal, a few weeks after I arrived. Some Japanese friends had arranged an outing to a celebrated restaurant which specialised in the dish which epitomises the pinnacle of Japanese cuisine - blowfish. This is a horrendously expensive delicacy, which can only be served by a specially licensed cook, because it is poisonous unless meticulously prepared. It is of course eaten raw, and is presented with great pomp and ceremony, beautifully arranged on ancient serving dishes, and exotically garnished.

We had had the preliminary courses, and the highlight of the meal was borne in. The whole fish was artistically displayed on a venerable platter, already cut in slices to the backbone, the head and tail disposed so as to give the illusion that it was leaping skywards from the green bed of garnish. There was a religious hush while everyone marvelled. Suddenly, the tail twitched - several times. I was petrified. I couldn't stop myself from exclaiming, "It's still alive!" One of the Japanese gave me a puzzled look. "Of course," he said, "How else could you be sure it's fresh?" Feeling quite light in the head, I asked, "you mean you cut it up while it's still living? Don't you knock it on the head first?" It was his turn to be shaken. Recovering himself, he replied in the tone of one whose disagreeable duty it is to reprove a friend. "But that would be cruel," he said.

Kate Mulvey

Amsterdam

Meg Moir

Long houses huddle and reflect.
Barges scape through tunnels.
Flower beds drift.

Gem cutters flaunt facets.
Tired bicycles
    lean on
Tired bicycles.

Feet tread marble steps,
wander from frame to frame.
Eyes search for captives,
caught by famous sons
held in a faded hue.

And in fields
giants stand alone,
hands and feet
    hurried
only by winds.

Salad
Days

She stood, tall, tanned, slender, and alone at one end of the swimming pool. Her toes curled over the edge, and the water below was green and smooth like a mirror. She dived into her own reflection and swam elegantly and rhythmically up the centre of the pool......

The dream faded and Emma reluctantly opened her eyes and peered short-sightedly through her sunglasses. The sun had moved while she slept and the strip of sand where she lay was now in the shadow of the cliff. A few late holidaymakers splashed at the water's edge but the beach was quiet. She struggled into a sitting position and glanced down at her dimpled thighs with a shiver of distaste. This holiday had been an expensive mistake — too late in the season, too few people of her own age, too many lonely days and evenings and too much rich and fattening food. Impatiently she heaved herself to her feet, but the effort made beads of sweat stand out on her brow causing her fringe to stick to her forehead. Down at the edge of the sea, the waves lapped an invitation, so she headed towards the water and waded gratefully into its welcoming coolness. In the water she looked different — she was different. Her plump arms arched gracefully and her heavy legs cleaved the water in a useful scissor kick. Soon she was well clear of the breakers and, turning on her back, she allowed herself to float dreamily, enjoying the warmth of the sun on her face.

A speedboat puttering in the distance did nothing to disturb her, but sweeping round the bay in a creamy curve, the water skier was almost on her before he knew it, and, in making a last minute swerve, he lost his balance and fell, a stray ski spinning off at an angle to hit Emma a glancing blow......

Some hours later she opened her eyes and quickly shut them again as a stabbing pain shot through her head. The crisp rustle of starched material, a soft footfall nearby, encouraged her to try once more, but slowly and carefully this time. She was lying on a high firm hospital bed, and the nurse who now bent over her regarded her with sympathetic eyes. A glass straw was put in her mouth, and she swallowed gratefully the soothing liquid.

As the days passed, she grew accustomed to the wires which fastened her fractured jaw and allowed only liquids between her braced teeth. Physiotherapists worked conscientiously on the torn muscles in her leg, and the frequent sun baths on the hospital verandah turned her normally pale skin to a fetching shade of golden tan. Best of all were the visits from the handsome water-skier, the cause of her present confinement. Daily he supplied her with books and magazines, flowers and fruit juices, and when at last she was released from hospital, she made no objection to her handsome visitor's firm proposal that she spend her convalescence in the luxurious villa, complete with swimming pool, which he shared with his parents.

And so later that same day, as she regarded her reflection in the full length mirror in her bedroom, she smiled. The weeks of enforced liquid diet, the daily massage of her limbs, and the frequent sun-bathing sessions had done their work. Putting on the new bathing suit, thoughtfully provided for her, she went outside and stood...... tall and tanned and slender on the edge of the swimming pool. The water below was green and smooth like a mirror. She dived into her own reflection and swam elegantly and rhythmically up the centre of the pool.

Jean McGregor

Message in a Bottle

Read this, you who find it. It might do you good. Especially if you sometimes get a little bit sick of yourself, or tired of a life that seems to encapsulate you. Things can change. Leopards, never mind what people say, can change their spots.

At fifty-nine I was thrown on the human scrap heap - forcibly retired - because of partial blindness, and chronic spinal arthritis. A lifelong workaholic and compulsive high achiever, I simply languished, cut off from my power source. I couldn't have done much anyway, because my spinal trouble kept me in pain, and flat on my back for weeks on end. Then, two years into retirement, and in the unexpected stress situation of a family bereavement, I suffered a heart attack.

An operation eased my heart problem, but the cumulative effect of these maladies was a crippling depression, which culminated in a six month period of prostration, in bed, at home, in traction. Then I was diagnosed as being diabetic. Life was pain-filled, wretched, and, as far as could be seen, hopeless.

One evening, filled with mutinous resentment, and looking like a wrathful ghost, I forced myself out of bed to watch the Choir-Of-The-Year competition on television. And Lo! There was a Barbershop Chorus singing in that competition. I am not sure of what happened. Maybe it was the infectious happiness of the men singing; maybe I was so low down that the only way was up. Whatever the reasons, I began to feel better. My wife says I actually smiled.

Next day I wrote to that chorus, thanking them for their effect on me. They wrote back, inviting my wife and myself to attend the National Convention two months later. We went, me hobbling on two sticks, and were submersed for two days in Barbershop singing, and determined happiness. I came home with a load of books on harmony, and started a Barbershop chorus locally, although I had never sung anywhere but in the bath.

I learned that the Senior Studies Institute ran a course called "Enjoy Your Voice", an introduction to singing. I attended, learned, and passed on what I knew, to the men in my new chorus. I was now walking without sticks, and singing without inhibitions.

Next I learned of the existence of the Alexander Technique, and borrowed books about it. One book said it could change one's life. I snorted a bit when I read that. But I saw, in the next edition of the University's brochure, a course entitled "An Introduction to the Alexander Technique". I enrolled, attended, and practised conscientiously. Slowly I learned important things about myself; mainly that, all my life, I had been going about my achieving the wrong way, and that my efforts were either bound to fail, or else put me on the human scrap heap. Which, of course, was what had happened.

I had, at nearly seventy, to go back to the beginning and learn to live in a different way. There was no alternative. Well, there was; I could go back to being chronically unwell. I chose to persevere with the Technique.

In 1995 I enrolled in another course of the Senior Studies Institute; Taijiquan & Qigong. Again books warned me that this study could change my life. I still did not believe it. That was foolish talk, irresponsible talk, dangerous talk.

Three months after starting the exercises, something is happening. I am not imagining it. There is a fundamental change in me, a personality change. I am a different man. I am well. I am at peace with myself. I am achieving things with a fraction of the effort I used to require. I am confident that I can do anything I might want to do. I realise that, for the first time in my history, I am positively enjoying living.

I don't know whether I have to thank Barbershop singing, or The Alexander Technique, or Taiji Qigong: I suspect that the change is a result of a combination of all three disciplines. I can't explain how the miracle works. This would have bothered me once. It doesn't now. All my life, until three years ago, I banked everything on logic, on science, on reason. It wasn't a good bet. Now, more and more, I let my body decide things.

One thing I do know: all my early, and middle age, learning was learning about **subjects**: I was learning to pass exams, or I was acquiring the stock-in-trade information which I would pass on to other people as a means of earning a living. My recent, recuperative learning has been learning about **me** — about what I've got inside me, how I can best use it, and what-do-I-want-to-do-with-it.

If I was a one-off case, this wouldn't matter much. However, I work a good deal with people nowadays, retired people, redundant people, unemployed people. They are not all fulfilled, liberated personalities. I recognise in many of them the fears and doubts that so restricted me throughout the greater part of my life; the crippling inhibitions that stifle real ability; the fears of success and failure that deny one the realisation of potential; the self-imposed iron clamps that often imprison the creative force in individuals. These people have all had some education; they have learned things, and this learning has enabled them, like myself, to earn a living, but it hasn't done much to develop them as individual human beings.

It needn't always be like that. People can always learn, and change, and perhaps later life is the best time for it. Retirement may provide the time. A lifetime's failure may provide the stimulus, and the preciousness of the time remaining may provide the motivation.

If others are as lucky as I am, they might realise that the best opportunities are not necessarily enjoyed by youth. For some, the good wine has truly been kept for the last.

John McGeough

A
Terminal
Disease

Age is a terminal disease, the doctor said,
folding his bored, unwrinkled hands,
his gaze dismissive.

I reach for the prescription
trying to hide my liver-spotted hands,
and find myself outside with all unsaid.

Home bandages the wound.
Soothed by small familiar tasks,
fear ebbs away, until
I glance outside and see
crows sitting, rusty-black.

Muriel Kitchener

The
Glasgow
Aunts

They talked
And found no contradiction,
Looked in each others' eyes
And were reflected back.

Still in their parents' home
They carried on
A conversation that began
Before their births.

They sat between tall
Chests-of-drawers in shadows that
Had thrown the self-same shapes
For eighty years of
Calvinistic certainty.

They lived their youth
And their maturity,
Then died, and in
A Covenanting heaven carry on
The family conversation.

Moyra McGavin

Cuillins

Tall old women
stand,
mist-shawls drooped
over stooped shoulders,
swathed about heathery skirts.

White caps nod together
whispering,
listening to tales of
a time before time,
when tall old women were young.

Pat Irvine

A Matter of Style

"Is this seat taken?" I scarcely raised my eyes from my book.

"It doesn't appear to be," I replied, "But then, neither are most of the seats in this carriage."

"Ah, but this is the one I fancy!"

It was a young man's voice, light but with a disconcertingly personal note to it. I glanced at him over the tops of my half-moon spectacles, as he settled himself opposite me.

"Even in these outrageous times," I commented, "I hardly imagine that your motive in changing seats at this late stage in the journey is to ...... chat me up, as I believe they say nowadays."

"My god! You're Miss Paton. You can't be. You must have died years ago. I mean, she must have...... But you are, aren't you? Miss Paton! That's amazing!"

"Paton is my name, and I am not dead yet, incredible though it may seem to you. I am often rather surprised about it myself. However, I'm still in possession of most of my faculties. As you see, I'm still mobile and still literate, even when it comes to an avant-garde novel, such as this." I waved the book in my hand, not attempting to hide my impatience to return to it, but courtesy, if not curiosity, demanded something of me first.

"And you are a former pupil? Let me see now ......"

"Ross MacIntyre. Don't you recognise me? I suppose it's difficult. I was a spotty, gauche, ugly adolescent when you last saw me."

I was now giving him my whole attention. Older than I had first imagined, he certainly merited none of these self-disparaging adjectives now.

"You have improved," I said judiciously. He laughed then, suddenly and heartily. I had forgotten how disarming a young man's laughter could be.

"And you haven't changed at all," he said. "It's still '19 out of 25. Imaginative content, but sloppy punctuation.' "

I remembered him then, among the hundreds, seeing in the man's face the boy he had been, a bubble of leaven in the dough of V(B), that last year of my teaching; leaven which worked along with me to lift the whole.

"Tell me," he continued, indicating the book with its distinctive stark cover-design, which now lay face-downwards on my lap, "Are you enjoying your book?"

"I was. Very much."

"Before I interrupted you? Sorry. But I know this book. It seems a strange choice. I wouldn't have thought......."

"You feel it might shock me, aged spinster and retired schoolmistress that I am? Hardly. Why does your generation think it invented sex? What about Joyce, Lawrence, even Radcliffe Hall? Shocked I am not! And please do not patronise me, Ross Macintyre!"

To my surprise, I heard in my voice the tone of the classroom, last used many years ago, and I imagined I saw him flinch slightly before he apologised. Recovering quickly, he returned to the subject of my choice of reading.

"You think this book's well written? A good read?"

"Both of these things. My great-niece told me it was quite un-put-downable, and I've been forced to keep putting it down all weekend. Quite frustrating, but it would be very rude to give the impression that a book is more fascinating than the people one's visiting. Yes, for a first novel, it's exceptionally good. The plot seems a little contrived but the characters are so good, it hardly matters. It's Scottish, too. One mustn't be chauvinistic, of course, but a new Scots writer of this calibre — well, it's an added pleasure. No wonder the critics are enthusiastic."

"But the style? Do you like the style? You were always hot on style." A memory flash-back took me over fifteen years.

"And you had many, Ross Macintyre. A different one for every piece of writing. MacCaig one day, the next Amis, father or son."

"And you told me, find your own voice, and you may someday write something worth reading."

The rhythm of the train's wheels changed as we approached Waverley Station. I closed my book thoughtfully, and carefully placed my spectacles in their case. I thought of my great-niece, and of her animation as she recommended the book to me.

"You haven't explained yet why you came to sit opposite me. You didn't recognise me till after you'd moved."

He smiled. "You know, don't you?"

"I think so." I held up the book. " 'Roderick Macleod.' A pseudonym, isn't it? I suppose that to a writer his own book is instantly recognisable, even down the length of a railway carriage."

"I couldn't resist it. It's still such a thrill to see someone actually reading my book! You must think me very big-headed......"

"Not in the least."

I began to assemble my belongings, almost with regret. He was a very charming companion.

"23 out of 25," I added. "An excellent piece of work."

We were still laughing when the train drew to a halt.

"Let me help you," he offered.

About to refuse in my usual over-independent manner, I thought better of it. "How kind," I replied. "If you could take this small case. But I'll slow you down. Is someone meeting you, perhaps? Your wife or girlfriend......"

As he helped me off the train, he looked rueful for the first time. "Nothing in that department at the moment."

I thought again of my delightful great-niece who would be waiting for me. Firmly, I took my companion's arm. "Come along," I told him. "I want you to meet one of your fans......"

Elderly spinster I may be, and certainly not addicted to romantic fiction, but even I can recognise the perfectly matched couple. It's simply a matter of style.

Janet McKenzie

A Ripple
On The
Pool

He left the train and made his way out of the station, his feeling of confidence increasing as he caught more than one admiring female glance. He strode purposefully along, occasionally catching glimpses of his pleasing reflection in large plate glass windows along the way. His mind was busy with thoughts of the coming interview and how best to display his many talents.

At one point he was approached by a girl with an armful of magazines, but he regally sailed past. Then as he waited at the traffic lights, he was aware of the girl again. His glance was brief and dismissive.

He pressed on to his destination and entered the imposing portals of the famous school. The interview went very well, and the members of the panel seemed impressed by his undeniably excellent academic qualifications and his considerable educational experience. The questions about ethos and relationships, about the welfare of pupils, and about their development as whole human beings, were easy to answer and elaborate on. After all, he did have a way with words and was used to producing what was expedient. He left with a smile on his face, his confidence and self-satisfaction undented.

A strange thing happened as he crossed the road. He saw the girl again. Momentarily he felt slightly uneasy but this quickly passed as he made his way through the crowds to the station. He stopped to buy a newspaper and as he did so he felt a hand on his arm. It was the girl.

"What do you want?" he asked abruptly.

"Don't you know me? I was one of your pupils a few years ago," she said.

Somewhat taken aback, he looked more closely at her but could find nothing in the old young face to remind him of the schoolgirl she must once have been.

"What's brought you to this?" he asked rather self righteously.

"I had a crush on you. I thought you were wonderful and could do no wrong. Remember the debates we had in class? You were so clever and could subtly ridicule our ideals and beliefs. You couldn't resist trying to influence our thinking with your smooth talk. Over the year when I was in your class I began to believe that I was a free spirit, like a god who needed no rules, no restraints. When I left school I threw overboard the standards of my family and left home."

There was silence. The girl looked at him. He felt shaken. All the euphoria of his day had gone. It was an incredible situation - how dare she do this to him? What did she want? Not that he owed her anything of course.

Then he breathed a sight of relief. He knew what to do. He turned the full battery of his smile upon her and graciously bought one of her magazines.

Edith Fotheringham

Temper, Temper!

As I get older, I become more and more petulant, more petty, more easily ruffled. Or so I am told. But I'm not too sure, for I am a well balanced sort of chap.

Perhaps the cause is that I am very conscious that time is no longer on my side. If I am anything at all, I am ambitious, wanting to do things that I should have done years ago. One of these is to write professionally. For money, that is. I do not exactly need the money, for my needs are limited and my income adequate, but those who know tell me that the satisfaction comes from the challenge to convince an editor that your stuff is worth publishing.

Consequently, when I go to a class to study writing, I am very eager to learn the tricks of the trade. I want the tutor to guide me in all its aspects, to read my work critically and comment constructively. Naturally, I am less than interested in the aspirations of my fellow students. Their work, and my tutor's attention to it, interferes with my progress. Some of the other students are stupid. They will never become writers, so they should just go away and leave the tutor to me. Others are so good they do not need the advice of the tutor. They attend the class merely to demonstrate how clever, how accomplished, they are. I hate them.

The tutor must always be on time. On this I insist. If the tutor is late I do not want to know why. I want him to know just how unsatisfactory this is, and that it must never be repeated, for I am being inconvenienced. Another thing. I have not come for social chit chat. No, I have come to learn, for I have much to impart to the world and so little time in which to do it. Tutors are reluctant to see this obvious fact. Firstly, they seem to have the opinion that I have very little of worth to give out and secondly, they think there is all the time in the world in which to do it.

I look for good hand-outs from the tutor, but these will never be a substitute for skilled teaching. The imparting of knowledge at classes is, *per se*, both verbal and written. One has to be balanced against the other. It is not good enough to issue a few hand-outs, then rest on one's laurels for the rest of the two hours of that class. No, thank you.

If the tutor sets me work for the following week, and I do that work, I expect it will be examined in detail at the next class. There must be no shortcuts taken by the tutor, no stopping me in full flow to make some inane suggestion. No leaving my second submission until there is insufficient time to consider it carefully, and no "would you please read it out quickly, as we all want to get home." Not good enough, sir. And no stupid coffee breaks mid-class because some frivolous old woman says she is suffering caffeine withdrawal symptoms. My time is too precious for that.

When it is apparent that the tutor is making friends with the others, but ignoring me, I am a little puzzled. Like them I have paid my money. Then I realise, money cannot buy friendship. What can he see in them that I lack? I work hard and the quality of my work is first class. I am always civil to him, and only occasionally do I criticise him in class. I am entitled to do this, for I am the senior member of the class and with seniority must go some privilege.

And when others in the class seem to have benefited from the tuition and are now having their work published while mine continues to be rejected, that, too, is not good enough. Obviously, this is the fault of the tutor who has not adapted his technique to meet my needs. I'll have a word with him about that.

Better still, I will try a new tutor. That is now nine in a row who have failed me.

Andrew Hamilton

A Christmas Tail: (A Trifling Matter)

See Christmas, See Christmas dinner, could see it far enough.

You don't mean that!

It's all that preparation and the worry that things turn out all right.

I see what you mean. I had a **very** worrying Christmas dinner a few years back that still sends shivers up and down my spine.

What happened?

I couldn't possibly tell you — I haven't told a soul — don't dare.

Go on — you can tell me — I won't breathe a word.

Well — if you promise — here, have another biscuit — home baked. There I was busy clearing the table after the turkey and trimmings. I had the dirty dishes piled on the tray and had invited the others to pass round the Muscatel in readiness for the sweet.

Your famous trifle?

Right — with Cointreau and mandarin oranges. There was only the one choice because nobody ever wants anything else but that trifle.

Mm-mm

So there I was, opening the door with one foot and balancing the tray on my hip — when I saw it.

What?

Away at the end of the hall, just inside the kitchen door — a tail — at table top level, wagging fit to drop off.

What do you mean — a tail?

What you find on the end of a dog. In this case a black and tan one, just like the one on our 12 week old pup.

Oh no ! Not your.....?

I raced up that hall as fast as my loaded tray would allow — like some demented cinema usherette — and if you've ever tried screaming aloud silently — I was doing that as well.

Did nobody else know what was going on?

They were too busy enjoying my Muscatel. Mind you, some well meaning busybody shouted out "Need a hand?" and I had to answer "No thanks, everything's under control!"   Under control?   Everything was under the dog! There it was up to its scruff in pure dairy cream, scrabbling furiously through the mandarins, lapping the Cointreau at the bottom and all the while that tail wagging in a frenzy of ecstasy.

Oh my Lord — what did you do?

I dumped the dishes, yanked that tail and its owner out of my trifle, threw open the door and hurled it into the night.

Did it not protest?

Protest ? Not a whimper. It was incapable. When everybody was leaving around midnight we found it lying where it had landed — in a drunken stupor and frozen solid in the snow. We only knew it was there by its tail sticking straight up like a periscope. We had to defrost it in front of the fire — but not too near, you know?

Then what?

Then I hopped around having a silent nervous breakdown, punching the air at an imaginary pup and screaming inwardly "Why me, God?" Pure pantomime.

But what did you serve for a sweet ?

My trifle.

You didn't!

Dire straits demand dire remedies, friend. I had no other option. I offered a quick prayer to the Gods of Cordon Bleu of the desperado kind, creamed off the top layer, poured out a glass of Cointreau, dribbled half into the trifle and drank the rest. I used the cream held back for Boxing Day and sprinkled the remains of the jelly fruits sachet on the top, and then I tangoed up the hall with the tarted up trifle — if you'll excuse the expression.

Did nobody — I mean — were there no after effects? Did you get away with it?

Well — you were there! Another biscuit ?

Mary McLevey

Gotlib, Steelhenge, and The Telly

It's funny how certain years stand out in the memory. Such a one for me was 1971. Can it be a quarter of a century ago? I was appointed Director of Extension Studies (in addition to the post that I already held as Professor of Biology) and it was certainly a wide remit!

Gotlib

The phone call, on 16th March, came from the Principal's Office. "This is Sam Curran. Mr Jack Nowell is the owner of 31 paintings and 22 drawings by the distinguished Polish artist, the late Hendrik Gotlib, and he has intimated in the press that he is willing to give these, on an extended loan, to British universities. Application has to be made to Mrs Gotlib who houses them. How soon can you be there?"

The next morning I was knocking at Mrs Gotlib's cottage door in the heart of Surrey. I was the first representative, by a long way, of all the universities and it gave great satisfaction, as we sat down to lunch together, that we were constantly interrupted by phone calls (including one from Edinburgh University) from people trying to make appointments.

Mrs Gotlib, a charming lady, and I hit it off rather well together — so much so that she allowed me to choose five paintings and three drawings for Strathclyde. That left 26 paintings and 19 drawings to be divided among the other 24 universities who had expressed interest. So we took possession of 'White Calf', 'Self Portrait with Dog', 'Kneeling Nude', 'Nude with 'Outstretched Arms', 'Self Portrait with Pipe', 'Portrait of Dorothy Nowell', 'Nude with Hand on Shoulder', and 'Standing Nude'. I agree that there are rather a lot of nudes among that lot but I was later pleased to read that, in the opinion of at least one art expert, Gotlib's nudes were the best paintings and drawings that he ever did. Mrs Gotlib later paid a visit to the University to view the paintings and to have lunch with the Principal, a few members of staff, the artist Emilio Coia, and Benno Schotz the sculptor.

The Principal bought another Gotlib, 'Workers at Noon' for the University. I last saw it hanging above the staircase at Ross Priory.

Steelhenge

Two months after visiting Mrs Gotlib, I was on my way south again, this time to London, to represent the University at the Arts Council Headquarters, Piccadilly, where the model of the proposed 'Steelhenge' (inspired by the Callanish stone circle in the Isle of Lewis), by the sculptor

Gerald Laing, would be revealed to the press (and to me!) for the first time. I made a wee speech and was quoted as saying that "we at Strathclyde are very excited at the thought of this magnificent Laing sculpture coming to our University". In return I got a magnificent lunch at 'Mirabelle' which included a bottle of Chateau Lamartine.

Later in the year the sculpture of some 14 pieces, some of them over 16ft. in height, covering an area of 30,000 square feet, was erected where Balmanno Brae levels off facing Cathedral Street. The pieces were cast at Ravenscraig, Motherwell, where more than three tons of steel were incorporated into the new alloy, Cor-ten steel. The total cost was £10,000 shared equally between the University and the Arts Council.

The Strathclyde Seminars

The Telly was a powerful force in those days, and it occurred to me that one way to publicise Strathclyde was to put it on the screen. And so, in February 1971, the 'Strathclyde Seminars' came into being. I discussed the format with the Head of S.T.V. who was keen that his company should transmit some up-market stuff. In all we put out six programmes (in colour !). We had a core of four Strathclyders - the Principal, Professors Howe and Kenedi and myself; two visiting Professors – Tom Gibson (surgeon) and Esmond Wright (historian) – and some distinguished 'outsiders' including Tony Benn MP (then Minister of Technology) and Lord Bowden (Principal of the Manchester Institute of Science and Technology). The overall theme was 'The Impact of Technology'. Each programme consisted of a 20 minute introductory talk by one of the participants, and topics included Higher Education, The Environment, Democracy, Technology, and Medicine, followed by an open-ended, unscripted, discussion.

I remember that the programmes were put out rather late on Sunday evenings. My wife got our little daughter Marion out of bed to watch her Dad in action. Her comment at the end of the programme was revealing; "Thank goodness that's over. Now I can get back to my bed!"

Bill Fletcher

The Bird in The Attic

"Something's up there." So far as Mrs McNee was concerned, this was a statement of fact, rather than a question.

She stood in the long hall of my flat, one arm resting on the vacuum cleaner, the other on her hip, speaking to my retreating back as I walked towards the lounge at the end of the passageway.

This small, shapely women, with a pert, heavily made-up face, had dark eyes and a cascade of black curls fluttering down long past her shoulder blades. Wearing a tight mini dress and high-heeled shoes, she resembled her own description of "cleaning person" far more accurately than my advertised "char lady", her only condescension to this title being the little pink apron she wore, which in itself was better suited to a French maid than a traditional British cleaning lady. However, during the three months I had employed her in my new home, the floors stayed clean and the furniture sparkled, so I had no reason to dismiss her.

"Yes sir, something's up there," Mrs McNee was now repeating. "There's a funny stain on the bathroom ceiling, sort of speckled and dark brown in colour." She screwed up her face in an effort to remember her timetable of events that led to this statement. "Well, Mr Bishop, when I arrived on Monday, I noticed the splatters and tried to wash them off, but this didn't work, so when I came on Wednesday, I used the small tin of emulsion kept in the cleaning cupboard and painted over the stains."

She paused, waiting to see if I had any comments to make. When I remained silent, she continued with the narrative. "Then, would you believe, when I came in this morning, I noticed the stains had reappeared!" Not only did she sound surprised, but affronted that the ceiling had dared defy her and reassert its brown blemishes.

As I still offered no suggestions, she remarked, "So you see, sir, something's definitely up there and you must go into the loft to discover what it is."

Whilst speaking to me, Mrs McNee had put away the Hoover and was enveloping herself in her fur-collared top coat, ready for the off.

"I expect it's a spilt tin of paint, or perhaps a dead bird?" suggested Mrs McNee as she approved her own outdoor reflection in the hallstand mirror.

I stood in the large lounge, gazing through the big picture window, looking down at the retreating weekend traffic of the small busy town, which seemed, through the expensively double-glazed glass, mute, as though determined not to intrude on my privacy.

Promotion had led me to this new town, where I had taken up residence in the luxury block within which I occupied the top floor apartment and, consequently, owned the attic space above. It was to this attic that Mrs McNee referred and it was something in this attic which was causing her this consternation.

"I'll go up and check it," I remarked absently as my eyes strayed to the Chesterfield couch and the headlines of the national newspaper lying thereon, which proclaimed the police were still searching for the man who had assaulted and murdered eight women in the large metropolis from whence I had recently arrived.

"That's fine then." Mrs McNee sounded satisfied as she pulled on her gloves at the open front door. " 'Bye for now then, see you next week and if you get the stain mystery solved, I'll be able to fix the ceiling on Monday morning." "Goodbye Mrs McNee, see you Monday," I replied as the door closed behind her.

Alone now in my luxuriant turret, my eyes wandered to the ceiling above. Mrs McNee was correct, there was "something up there." But it was neither paint nor bird; something more sinister reposed on those floorboards overhead. Unfortunately, my move to this new town had done nothing to stem the flow of a murderous, sexual appetite and I had already crushed my first victim. Now, contemplating Mrs McNee's early demise on Monday, I reflected sadly that there was and always would be "Something Up There."

Jean Freeman

Life
After
Life

Mary smoothed down her titanium skirt and regarded her perfect legs with smug satisfaction. They really had made a good job of them. She had to laugh when she remembered her first hip replacement, way back in the nineties; a great success at the time without doubt, but now? Well, these whole leg transplants were something else! No unsightly veins, just perfect, smooth, lightly tanned, blemish-free legs in the Betty Grable mode, because of course she had been allowed to choose the shape she wanted from quite a large selection.

She pirouetted in front of the mirror with a little laugh of sheer delight. She DID look good! Everything she had was now either rejuvenated or replaced. She was a new woman! Giving a final flick to her blonde bob, she glanced at the clock on the mantelpiece below the framed telegram from the Queen, and sashayed to the door. Time to meet that nice young man from downstairs — well, eighty-seven WAS young nowadays!

Jean McGregor

*Some of the writers gathered outside
The Senior Studies Institute*

BIOGRAPHIES OF AUTHORS

Ercell Carruthers graduated from the Open University in 1992. She lives in Blairgowrie, and is a member of the local Writers' Group.

Winifred Conway is a Scot "by adoption". She is interested in issues concerning older people, and in writing.

Pamela Duncan is a pillar of Eastwood Writers, and has published much of her work. She has studied Creative Writing for several years at Further Education classes.

Bill Fletcher has had a distinguished academic career, and is well known for his many publications, notably the recent "Baxter's Book Of Famous Scots Who Changed The World".

Edith Fotheringham is from Glasgow. She has attended Art Classes locally, and is currently studying Creative Writing with S.S.I.

Jean Freeman describes herself as "Chapelhall's only cockney". She has worked all over the world. Now retired, she studies with S.S.I.

Elisabeth Fry was born and raised in South Germany, and came to Scotland in 1955. Her first class with the S.S.I. was "Reading Scottish Writers". Elisabeth's story "THE SHOPPING TRIP" has been chosen as runner-up to the winning entry.

Andrew Hamilton began a successful career at Singers, Clydebank and completed it at Rolls Royce. Still eager to learn, he then worked for, and gained, an MA(Hons) at Glasgow University. He is now "striving to become a writer."

Pat Irvine is from Glasgow, and a recent graduate of the Open University. She has published a collection of poetry under the title "Green Moon Riding".

Betty Jack's original home is Aberdeenshire. She is a Volunteer Guide with the University of Strathclyde and is currently following classes in Singing and Exploring Glasgow.

Netta Jess has, like all true writers, held a number of varied positions in her working life. Now retired, she is a member of the Erskine Writers' Workshop.

Muriel Kitchener was born and brought up in London. She is currently working at clay sculpture in her local school, and is a member of Eastwood Writers.

Ellen Lamont has lived in Lochgoilhead for many years. She helped to start up Lochgoilhead Writers' Group, and has published some of her short stories.

Jean MacBeath hails from Cromarty. She has, for five years, worked with the Samaritans, and is a Trustee of Cromarty Courthouse Museum.

Moyra McGavin says that she is "by birth half-East and half-West coast; perhaps an uneasy mixture". She has written some children's books. Moyra now lives on the Isle of Bute, and belongs to the local Writers' Group. Her poem, "THE GLASGOW AUNTS" has been chosen as the winning entry to VOICES OF EXPERIENCE.

John McGeough earned his living playing dance music and jazz, then qualified as a teacher of English in 1970. Nowadays, he is particularly interested in the process of learning, and its effects on human beings.

Jean McGregor, received an Honours degree from the Open University in 1990. She is at present studying Creative Writing with the S.S.I.

Elizabeth MacLean was an engineer in the shipyard during the war. She writes, "After five years of studying to become a teacher, I found studying had become a habit, and took a B.A. course with the Open University." She is now retired and a member of the Erskine Writers' Workshop.

Mary McLevey stopped work as a teacher of French and Spanish in 1995, but still is passionately interested in language and travel. Mary is from Uddingston, and has studied Calligraphy with the S.S.I.

Janet McKenzie has "always enjoyed writing", and has published serials, articles, prose, and poetry. She is currently President of Perthshire Writers' Group, and is a founder member of the Blairgowrie Writers' group, both of which evolved from Adult Education classes.

Helen McLuckie has studied Art, Creative Writing, and Spanish in various Adult Education Centres, and is a member of the Royal Scottish Geographical Society.

Meg Moir has recently spent three years studying Classical Civilisations at Glasgow University. After many years in Warwickshire, Meg is now a Merchant City dweller.

Nada Mooney belongs to Glasgow, is a member of a local Writers Group, and has had three short stories published.

Margaret Morgan has always lived in Glasgow. She is a member of the 3Ls Writers Group, and this is the first time her work has been published.

Kate Mulvey is Glaswegian, though much of her life has been spent in other countries. Her great interest is language, and "the means by which each race seeks to reach the goals and deal with the problems we all have in common." Kate relies on the stimulus of a writing class for encouragement and discipline.

Jack Paul is from Irvine, and made his living with the merchant Navy. A change of direction in the sixties led to a BSc. and a second career as a Geography Lecturer. Now retired, Jack has studied Video Production and Creative Writing with S.S.I.

Sheila Rees finds the Creative Writing Group near her home in Arran ready with "mutual support which is helpful and stimulating." Sheila's aim is to chronicle her life for the next generation.

Phyllis Smart, a Glaswegian, relaxes by "putting cold teabags on her eyes and listening to 'The Pearl Fishers' sung by Jussi Bjorling and Robert Merrill." Phyllis joined Carl MacDougall's S.S.I. class in Creative Writing three years ago, and is "thoroughly hooked."

Iain Turner's working life has been in newspapers, as a linotype operator. He lives in Erskine, and is especially interested in writing and local history.

Heather Bruyere Watt lives in Lochgoilhead, and has been "an inveterate scribbler since schooldays". She has completed a play, and is now working on her first novel.

Moyra McGavin; Winner

Further copies of **Voices of Experience** may be obtained from
The Senior Studies Institute, Graham Hills Building,
40 George St., Glasgow G11QE
Tel 0141 552 4400 ext 2938

Is it too Late?

Is it too late?   Ah, nothing is too late
Till the tired heart shall cease to palpitate.
Cato learnt Greek at 80; Sophocles
Wrote his grand Oedipus, and Simonedes
Bore off the prize of verse from his compeers,
When each had numbered more than fourscore years.........

What then?   Shall we sit idly down and say
The night hath come;   it is no longer day?
The night hath NOT yet come;   we are not quite
Cut off from labour by the failing light;
Something remains for us to do or dare;
Even the oldest tree some fruit may bear;........
For age is opportunity no less
Than youth itself, though in another dress,
And as the evening twilight fades away
The sky is filled with stars, invisible by day.

*An excerpt from "**Morituri Salutamus**"*
by Henry Wadsworth Longfellow

SENIOR STUDIES
INSTITUTE

What *is* The Senior Studies Institute?

It is a University institution providing stimulating daytime classes for the over 50s. It also strives to create opportunities for older people to become achievers in the fields of learning, volunteering, or work, enabling them to remain a valuable resource for the community.

What is special about our Classes?

- ◆ Students are all in the 50+ age group with an interesting range of life experience.
- ◆ They offer a wide range of topics of special interest to mature people, including art, computer studies, current affairs, health maintenance, languages, literature and social studies.
- ◆ Classroom practises reflect the way that adults learn providing a supportive learning environment.
- ◆ Accreditation is an option within certain classes and there is also the opportunity for under-graduate study.
- ◆ Enjoying learning is at the heart of the experience.

Other activities.

❏ **Study trips and travel opportunities.** Places of local interest, European destinations and further afield.

❏ **Lunchtime meetings on current affairs.** Speaking out on issues of concern.

❏ **Volunteer Training.** By tapping into people's skills and life experience, the SSI offers specialist training in various kinds of volunteering activities.

❏ **Research** into Third Age issues.

Learning in
Later Life
Students' Association

What *is* The Learning in Later Life Students' Association?

◆   It is a democratic voluntary
     association run by an elected
     management council of 3L
     students.

◆   It is open to everyone who is a present
     student or has attended a class at SSI.

◆   It organises a stimulating social
     programme and student exchange,
     including excursions and travel
     opportunities to places of local
     interest, European destinations and
     further afield.

◆   It runs 'Freshers' Afternoons for new
     students.

◆   It provides access to specialist clubs.
     These provide opportunities for
     informal study and continuing social
     contact at the end of class.

◆   It organises seasonal celebrations and
     commemorative lunches.

3L Clubs

Art • Body Maintenance • Bridge • French • German
Italian • Think Yourself Young • Spanish
Urban Walking • 3Ls Writers' Group
University Guiding Group • Tuesday Club

Other University Bicentenary Publications

❖ ❖ ❖ ❖ ❖

John Anderson's Legacy

Emeritus Professor John Butt, who was formerly Professor of Economic History at Strathclyde University, is the author of ***John Anderson's Legacy — The University of Strathclyde and its antecedents, 1796 – 1996***. This book, published by Tuckwell Press Ltd., tells the University's story from its visionary founder, John Anderson, to the many men and women who steer it towards the millenium.

250 pages, numerous colour and black-and-white illustrations, ISBN 1 898410 682. Price £14.99p plus postage — £1.00p U.K.; £1.50p abroad.

From: Tuckwell Press Ltd., The Mill House, Phantassie, East Linton, East Lothian, EH40 3DG; or External Affairs and Development, University of Strathclyde.

❖ ❖ ❖ ❖ ❖

Perspectives

This lavishly illustrated photographic record provides an up-to-date, though sometimes nostalgic, view of life at the University of Strathclyde — its campuses and buildings, its people and activities. For anyone who ever studied here, or taught, or even visited for a short while — it's a gift. To your son or daughter, your partner, your parents, or even to yourself.

Available, £20.00p per copy, from John Smith & Son (Glasgow) ltd., 100 Cathedral Street, Glasgow G1 Tel: 0141-552 3377 and other branches; or from External Affairs and Development, University of Strathclyde.

❖ ❖ ❖ ❖ ❖